7
9/14
2/21

EXPLORING DINOSAURS & PREHISTORIC CREATURES

TRILOBITES

By Susan H. Gray

THE CHILD'S WORLD®
CHANHASSEN, MINNESOTA

The
Child's
World®

Published in the United States of America by The Child's World®
PO Box 326, Chanhassen, MN 55317-0326
800-599-READ
www.childsworld.com

Content Adviser:
Brian Huber, PhD,
Curator, Department
of Paleobiology,
Smithsonian
National Museum
of Natural History,
Washington DC

Photo Credits: James L. Amos/Corbis: 16; Kevin Schafer/Corbis: 27; The Field Museum,
Neg #GEO80820c, Photographer Ron Testa: 4; Mike Fredericks: 14, 15, 20, 21, 23;
Roger Viollet/Getty Images: 11; the Natural History Museum, London: 6, 19, 22, 26;
Sinclair Stammers/Photo Researchers, Inc.: 5, 10; Gary Retherford/Photo Researchers,
Inc.: 12; Chase Studio/Photo Researchers, Inc.: 13; Sinclair Stammers/Science Photo
Library/Photo Researchers, Inc.: 18; Ken Lucas/Visuals Unlimited: 7, 17; Dr. Gary
Gaugler/Visuals Unlimited: 8; Tom Panteges/Visuals Unlimited: 25.

The Child's World®: Mary Berendes, Publishing Director

Editorial Directions, Inc.: E. Russell Primm, Editorial Director; Pam Rosenberg,
Line Editor; Katie Marsico, Associate Editor; Matthew Messbarger, Editorial Assistant;
Susan Hindman, Copy Editor; Melissa McDaniel, Proofreader; Tim Griffin/IndexServ,
Indexer; Olivia Nellums, Fact Checker; Dawn Friedman, Photo Researcher; Linda
S. Koutris, Photo Selector

Original cover art by Todd Marshall

The Design Lab: Kathleen Petelinsek, Design; Kari Thornborough, Page Production

Library of Congress Cataloging-in-Publication Data
Gray, Susan Heinrichs.
  Trilobites / by Susan H. Gray.
     p. cm. — (Exploring dinosaurs & prehistoric creatures)
  Includes index.
  ISBN 1-59296-369-2 (lib. bd. : alk. paper) 1. Trilobites—Juvenile literature. I. Title.
  QE821.G73 2005
  565'.39—dc22   2004018068

TABLE OF CONTENTS

CHAPTER ONE

4 Stop, Drop, and Roll

CHAPTER TWO

7 What Were the Trilobites?

CHAPTER THREE

11 An Incredible Group of Animals

CHAPTER FOUR

16 What Did Trilobites Do All Day?

CHAPTER FIVE

22 Rollin' Rollin' Rollin'

CHAPTER SIX

24 Trilobites Everywhere

28 Glossary

28 Did You Know?

29 How to Learn More

30 The Geologic Time Scale

32 Index

Stop, Drop, and Roll

The trilobite (TRY-lo-bite) scooted around at the base of the coral reef. As he moved, he waved his antennae and kept watch for signs of danger. His legs stirred up tiny water currents that swept bits of food toward his mouth. The seafloor was calm

A trilobite (center) scurries toward the shelter of some underwater rocks. Several thousand different types of trilobites swam in prehistoric oceans.

near the coral reef, and food

was plentiful.

Suddenly, a

shadow passed over.

With more than

10,000 lenses in each

eye, the trilobite could

not help but see it.

Immediately, he

The hardened remains of this trilobite reveal an animal that died while it was curled up in a tight ball. Even when rolled into this protective position, trilobites were able to keep a careful watch over what was going on around them.

stopped feeding. He drew his legs in toward his stomach and began to

curl up. He folded down his antennae and bent his head toward his tail-

piece until the two met. Within seconds, he became a tight little ball,

protected by his hard outer covering. He sat on the seafloor, not moving

a muscle. His eyes kept watch though, looking for further threats.

More than 400 million years ago, prehistoric oceans were filled with early forms of life. Scientists believe that most trilobites were bottom-dwellers that lived along the seafloor.

Several minutes passed and nothing happened. Several more minutes went by, and the trilobite opened up a little. He wiggled his legs a bit and waved his gills. The water was still calm, and it seemed safe to come out. Slowly, he straightened his body and stretched out his antennae. He popped his legs out to the sides and continued on his way.

CHAPTER TWO

WHAT WERE THE TRILOBITES?

Trilobites were animals that lived in the oceans from about 540 million to 245 million years ago. Most lived in warm, shallow waters. The word *trilobite* comes from Greek words that mean "three lobes." Trilobites were given this name because the middle part of each animal's body was divided into three parts called lobes.

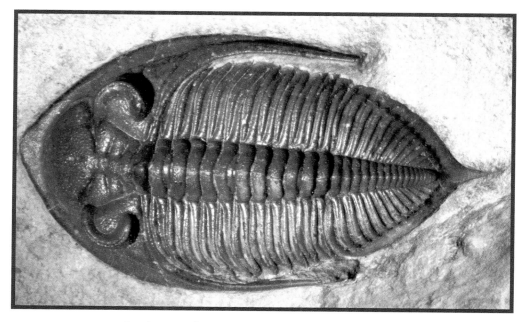

By the time dinosaurs existed on Earth, all that was left of trilobites were their hardened remains.

Wolf spiders are modern-day arthropods. Like their prehistoric ancestors, wolf spiders have exoskeletons.

Trilobites were arthropods (AR-thruh-podz). These are animals

with no backbones and with limbs that have joints. Modern-day

arthropods include insects, spiders, crabs, and shrimp. Arthropods have no bones to support their bodies. Instead, a hard covering on the outside supports the body and protects the soft organs. This kind of covering is called an exoskeleton (EX-o-SKEL-uh-tuhn).

When trilobites and other ancient arthropods died, sometimes parts of their bodies were preserved. These remains are called fossils (FAH-sulz). Most trilobite fossils are not the remains of organs, antennae, or legs. They are the remains of the animals' hard exoskeletons.

The trilobite body had three main parts. The head part is called the cephalon (SEFF-uh-lon). Behind this is the middle part, or thorax (THOR-ax). Behind the thorax is the tail part, or pygidium (py-JID-ee-um).

The thorax itself was divided lengthwise into three sections. These sections are called lobes. The thorax was made up of overlapping segments. Different kinds of trilobites had different numbers of segments.

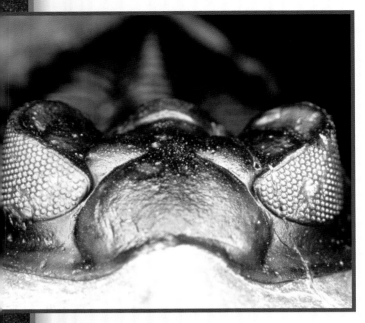

Many trilobites had excellent vision that allowed them to clearly view faraway objects.

The trilobite with the smallest number had only two segments. The one with the most had 61. Each segment had a pair of limbs—one on the right and one on the left. Each limb had two parts. There was a jointed leg part for walking and a feathery gill part for breathing.

Trilobites are the oldest animals known to have had eyes. Their eyes had many lenses, much like those of modern insects. Certain trilobites had hundreds of lenses in each eye, and some had thousands. Trilobites have been found that had four eyes, two eyes, and no eyes at all. The animals also had a pair of antennae for sensing things in the **environment.**

CHAPTER THREE

AN INCREDIBLE GROUP
OF ANIMALS

Trilobites were among the earliest animals that lived on Earth.

They survived for about 300 million years and spread every-

where. Then they died out right before the first dinosaurs appeared.

So far, scientists have found more than 15,000 different kinds of

Thanks to fossil remains, scientists discover new types of trilobites all the time.

Spiny trilobites discouraged predators looking for an easy meal.

trilobites. Their fossils show that they were an incredibly **diverse** group.

Most kinds of trilobites were about 1 to 2 inches (2.5 to 5 centimeters) in length. A few grew as long as 28 inches (71 cm). In some, the cephalon and pygidium were smooth and rounded. Others bore many spines, probably for defense. One kind of trilobite, *Ampyx* (AM-pix), had a long spine pointing forward from its cephalon and two pointing to the rear. These spines probably kept *Ampyx* from being eaten by other animals. Several types of trilobites were so well armored they even had spines on their spines!

Trilobite eyes came in all shapes and sizes. Some trilobites had eyes shaped like thin **crescents.** Others had huge, bulging eyes that could see things to the front, back, and sides. Still others had eyes at the ends of stalks. And little *Agnostus* (ag-NOSS-tus) had no eyes at all.

Trilobites had many different body shapes. In one group, the cephalon and pygidium made up almost the entire body. Some trilobites had very large cephalons with a huge swelling in the center. Some had a pygidium that ended in one or more long spines. Some trilobite bodies were long and narrow, while others were wide and flat.

Scientists believe that trilobites with no eyes lived in deep water where there was less light.

GOTTA GET OUT OF HERE

Like many modern-day arthropods, trilobites had to shed their exoskeletons as they grew. Unlike the skeleton of a human being, the exoskeleton of an arthropod cannot grow.

As an arthropod grows larger, it becomes packed more and more tightly inside its own body covering. Soon it has to break out. Therefore, animals with these hard outer coverings must shed them from time to time. This process is called molting (MOHLT-ing).

For an arthropod to molt, the exoskeleton has to crack apart. In trilobites, the exoskeleton cracked apart at weak lines on the cephalon. Then the trilobite struggled out of its old covering. For a while, the trilobite's new covering was soft. In time, though,

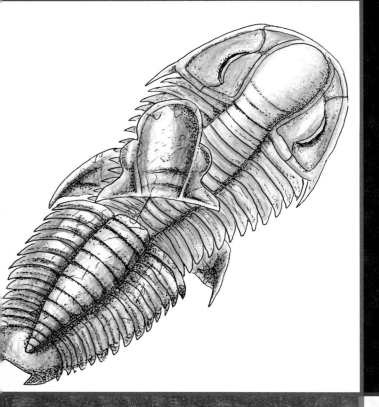

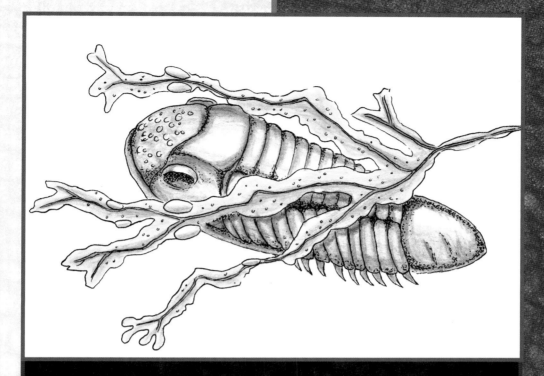

it hardened into a new protective exoskeleton— this one a little larger than the last. As long as it kept growing, a trilobite had to molt from time to time.

It was always danger-ous for a trilobite to molt. For a little while, the old exoskeleton covered the animal's eyes and made it impossible to see. Also, the trilobite probably dragged the exoskeleton for some time, trying to get out. This made it hard to move around. As soon as the trilobite was free, it had no real protection. Its soft, new exoskeleton was a poor armor against enemies. For these rea-sons, trilobites probably hid out in the seaweed or among coral shelters when molting.

CHAPTER FOUR

WHAT DID TRILOBITES
DO ALL DAY?

Trilobites spent much of their time moving around, feeding, and resting. Paleontologists (PAY-lee-uhn-TAWL-uh-jists) tell us that different trilobites had different ways of getting around and different ways of eating. Paleontologists are scientists who study **ancient** living things by looking at their fossils. The very best trilobite fossils show the animals' legs, heads, eyes, and mouth parts. Such things tell paleontologists a lot about how the creatures lived.

*Paleontologists have discovered trilobite
fossils on every continent.*

This trilobite had spines on its cephalon, thorax, and pygidium, in addition to spines on its legs.

Many trilobites lived on the ocean floor, walking along and searching for living or dead matter to eat. These trilobites had rough, spiny legs that could tear apart food and push it forward to the mouth. Some trilobites probably pulled worms from their **burrows,** tore them up, and moved the pieces into their mouths. Others probably

went along the floor, steadily pushing all kinds of small matter

toward the mouth, either to be swallowed or spit out.

Paleontologists think that certain trilobites moved along the

seafloor partly buried in the sand. These trilobites had eyes up on

stalks. They would have

been able to walk through

the sand and still see where

they were going.

Resting trilobites may

have found safety by scoot-

ing under a thin layer of

mud. With their flat bod-

ies, this would have been

*Like modern-day snails, some
trilobites had eye stalks.*

Some trilobites probably fed on tiny plants and animals that floated by on ocean currents.

easy to do. It would also have been an excellent way to rest, hidden

away from predators.

There were probably some trilobites that did not spend their lives

on the seafloor. Some may have been small and light enough to float

and drift along in the water. Maybe they could even steer a little by

moving their legs or gills. These trilobites would have fed on tiny

plants and animals that drifted along with them.

GROWING UP A TRILOBITE

Paleontologists believe that trilobites—like other arthropods—laid eggs. They don't know how many eggs were laid at a time. They also do not know if the parents cared for the eggs or if they just laid them and left.

A tiny, newly hatched trilobite looked nothing like its parents. It was not clearly divided into cephalon, thorax, and

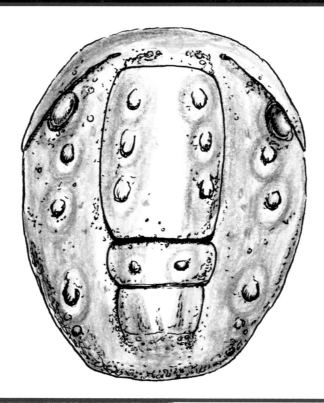

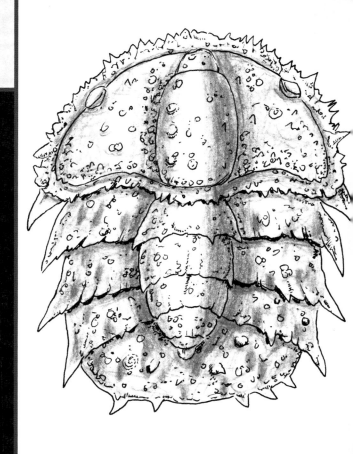

pygidium. Instead, it was a smooth, rounded, little creature. It had an exoskeleton and needed to molt as it grew.

As a trilobite grew, its looks changed. After molting a few times, the young trilobite's body had a little cephalon, thorax, and pygidium. The thorax was divided into lobes and had a couple of segments. Still, the trilobite did not look quite like an adult.

After a few more molts, a trilobite started looking like its parents. It developed spines, eye lenses, rough places on its legs, and long antennae. It continued to grow and molt until it reached adult size. Some of the largest trilobites molted more than 20 times before they were fully grown. Paleontologists tell us that most trilobite fossils are probably not the remains of the actual trilobite animals. They're really the molted exoskeletons that the animals left behind.

CHAPTER FIVE

ROLLIN' ROLLIN' ROLLIN'

People often find fossils of trilobites that are all rolled up. Their head and tail parts are nearly locked together. Why were these animals in such odd positions?

Most trilobites were able to curl up into a ball—a process called enrollment (en-ROHL-muhnt). Trilobites enrolled whenever they sensed danger. It was their way of protecting themselves.

When a trilobite enrolled, it bent over until its pygidium and cephalon met. Its body became a hard ball with only the exoskeleton showing. The legs, gills, and organs

When a trilobite enrolled, only the hard exoskeleton was visible to predators.

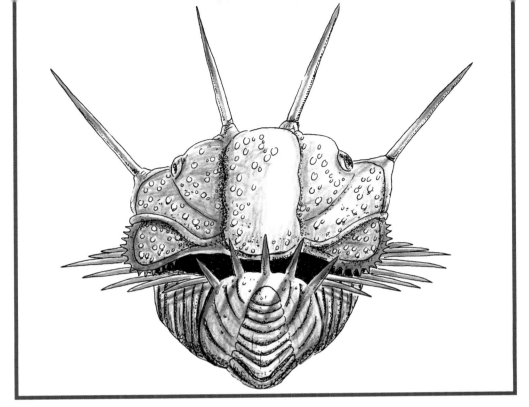

When spiny trilobites enrolled, predators were not likely to bother them.

were safely tucked inside the ball. In some trilobites, the edges of the

pygidium and cephalon had matching notches so they could tightly

clamp together. An enrolled trilobite would hold that clamped position

until the threat was gone.

Some trilobites had sharp spines on their bodies. When they

enrolled, the spines pointed outward. This was the perfect defense

against predators. Nothing would want to eat that hard ball of spines.

CHAPTER SIX

TRILOBITES EVERYWHERE

Trilobites lived all over the world, and people find their fossils all the time. Some states, such as Ohio, Iowa, and New York, have "fossil parks" where people can come and hunt for fossils. In Utah, people can visit a rock **quarry** that is loaded with trilobites. Children and adults find trilobites there by the handfuls. These aren't the only places where the arthropods lived. Their fossils can be found just about anywhere.

In the last several years, people have made some remarkable finds. In 1998, some paleontologists in Canada were out searching for fossils. They spotted a piece of a huge trilobite, but they figured the rest of it was probably broken off or missing. Once they started to clean the rocks and dirt away, they could not

Paleontologists discovered these trilobite fossils in Canada's Yoho National Park.

believe their eyes. They saw that the whole trilobite was present.

They worked hard to dig up the trilobite without damaging it.

Finally, they saw they had a creature that was almost 28 inches

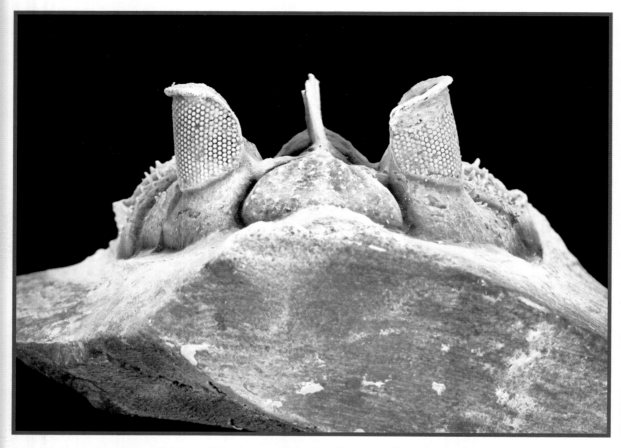

Erbenochile erbeni *is the scientific name of this unusual trilobite found in North Africa in 2003.*

(71 cm) long! This was the largest complete trilobite fossil ever found.

In 2003, scientists working in North Africa found a most unusual trilobite. This trilobite had eyes that stuck up like two small towers from its cephalon. The eyes were loaded with lenses that enabled the trilobite to see to the front, back, and sides all at once. What's more, each eye had an extra little part at the top that acted as a shade. Just like the brim of a baseball cap, this part kept the eye from getting too much light.

Trilobites were truly amazing creatures. They inhabited the oceans for 300 million years—nearly twice as long as the dinosaurs dominated the land. They crept along the seafloor and floated with the waves. They spread everywhere on Earth. Maybe some of them left fossils in your neighborhood.

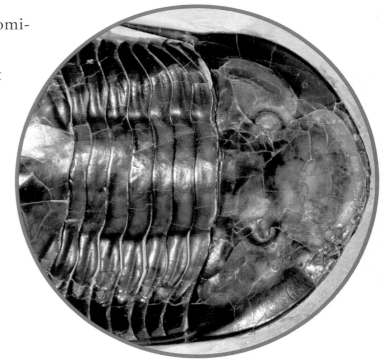

By studying trilobite fossils, paleontologists continue to learn more about these early arthropods and the role they played in prehistoric times.

Glossary

ancient (AYN-shunt) Something that is ancient is very old; from millions of years ago. Paleontologists study ancient life.

burrows (BUR-ohs) Burrows are tunnels or holes in the ground that are made by animals such as worms and rabbits. Some trilobites probably pulled worms from their burrows.

crescents (KRESS-uhnts) Crescents are things that are shaped like thin, curved slivers. Some trilobites had eyes shaped like crescents.

diverse (dye-VURSS) Diverse means having lots of differences. Trilobites were diverse in shape and size.

environment (en-VYE-ruhn-muhnt) The things that surround a living creature, such as the plants, air, and water, are its environment. The trilobites had a pair of antennae for sensing things in their environment.

quarry (KWOR-ee) A quarry is an open area where people obtain stones for roads and buildings. In Utah, people can visit a rock quarry that is loaded with trilobite fossils.

Did You Know?

▶ Scientists have found the artwork, tools, and jewelry of people who lived thousands of years ago in France. Among the pieces of jewelry are trilobite fossils with holes drilled in them. These were probably worn as necklaces.

▶ Trilobites were not the only animals to enroll. Pill bugs are small, gray arthropods that roll up whenever they are threatened. Some people call them roly-poly bugs.

▶ *Isotelus* (EYE-so-TEE-luss) was one of the largest trilobites, measuring up to 15 inches (38 cm) long and 10 inches (25 cm) wide. Many have been found in the United States. *Isotelus* is the state fossil of Ohio.

▶ Trilobites can be found all over the United States. To find the best places near you, contact the U.S. Geological Survey office closest to you.

How to Learn More

AT THE LIBRARY

Burns, Jasper. *Trilobites: Common Trilobites of North America.* Wilmington, Del.: Miller's Fossils, 1999.

Lambert, David, Darren Naish, and Liz Wyse. *Dinosaur Encyclopedia: From Dinosaurs to the Dawn of Man.* New York: Dorling Kindersley Publishing, 2001.

Palmer, Douglas, Barry Cox (editor). *The Simon & Schuster Encyclopedia of Dinosaurs & Prehistoric Creatures: A Visual Who's Who of Prehistoric Life.* New York: Simon & Schuster, 1999.

ON THE WEB

Visit our home page for lots of links about trilobites:
http://www.childsworld.com/links.html
NOTE TO PARENTS, TEACHERS, AND LIBRARIANS: We routinely verify our Web links
to make sure they're safe, active sites—so encourage your readers to check them out!

PLACES TO VISIT OR CONTACT

AMERICAN MUSEUM OF NATURAL HISTORY
To view numerous dinosaur fossils, as well
as the fossils of many ancient mammals
Central Park West at 79th Street
New York, NY 10024-5192
212/769-5100

CARNEGIE MUSEUM OF NATURAL HISTORY
To view a variety of dinosaur skeletons, as well
as fossils of other extinct animals
4400 Forbes Avenue
Pittsburgh, PA 15213
412/622-3131

KARL E. LIMPER GEOLOGY MUSEUM
To see trilobite fossils and learn more about these
extinct animals
Miami University
Oxford, OH 45056
513/529-3220

MUSEUM OF THE ROCKIES
To see real dinosaur fossils, as well as robotic replicas
Montana State University
600 West Kagy Boulevard
Bozeman, MT 59717-2730
406/994-2251 or 406/994-DINO (3466)

SMITHSONIAN NATIONAL MUSEUM
OF NATURAL HISTORY
To see several dinosaur exhibits and take special
behind-the-scenes tours
10th Street and Constitution Avenue NW
Washington, DC 20560-0166
202/357-2700

The Geologic Time Scale

CAMBRIAN PERIOD

Date: 540 million to 505 million years ago
Most major animal groups appeared by the end of this period. Trilobites were common and algae became more diversified.

ORDOVICIAN PERIOD

Date: 505 million to 440 million years ago
Marine life became more diversified. Crinoids and blastoids appeared, as did corals and primitive fish. The first land plants appeared. The climate changed greatly during this period—it began as warm and moist, but temperatures ultimately dropped. Huge glaciers formed, causing sea levels to fall.

SILURIAN PERIOD

Date: 440 million to 410 million years ago
Glaciers melted, sea levels rose, and Earth's climate became more stable. Plants with vascular systems developed. This means they had parts that helped them to conduct food and water.

DEVONIAN PERIOD

Date: 410 million to 360 million years ago
Fish became more diverse, as did land plants. The first trees and forests appeared at this time, and the earliest seed-bearing plants began to grow. The first land-living vertebrates and insects appeared. Fossils also reveal evidence of the first ammonoids and amphibians. The climate was warm and mild.

CARBONIFEROUS PERIOD

Date: 360 million to 286 million years ago
The climate was warm and humid, but cooled toward the end of the period. Coal swamps dotted the landscape, as did a multitude of ferns. The earliest reptiles existed on Earth. Pelycosaurs such as *Edaphosaurus* evolved toward the end of the Carboniferous period.

PERMIAN PERIOD

Date: 286 million to 248 million years ago
Algae, sponges, and corals were common on the ocean floor. Amphibians and reptiles were also prevalent at this time, as were seed-bearing plants and conifers. This period ended with the largest mass extinction on Earth. This may have been caused by volcanic activity or the formation of glaciers and the lowering of sea levels.

TRIASSIC PERIOD

Date: 248 million to 208 million years ago
The climate during this period was warm and dry. The first true mammals appeared, as did frogs, salamanders, and lizards. Evergreen trees made up much of the plant life. The first dinosaurs, including *Coelophysis*, existed on Earth. In the skies, pterosaurs became the earliest winged reptiles to take flight. In the seas, ichthyosaurs and plesiosaurs made their appearance.

JURASSIC PERIOD

Date: 208 million to 144 million years ago
The climate of the Jurassic period was warm and moist. The first birds appeared at this time, and plant life was more diverse and widespread. Although dinosaurs didn't even exist in the beginning of the Triassic period, they ruled Earth by Jurassic times. *Allosaurus, Apatosaurus, Archaeopteryx, Brachiosaurus, Compsognathus, Diplodocus, Ichthyosaurus, Plesiosaurus,* and *Stegosaurus* were just a few of the prehistoric creatures that lived during this period.

CRETACEOUS PERIOD

Date: 144 million to 65 million years ago
The climate of the Cretaceous period was fairly mild. Many modern plants developed, including those with flowers. With flowering plants came a greater diversity of insect life. Birds further developed into two types: flying and flightless. Prehistoric creatures such as *Ankylosaurus, Edmontosaurus, Iguanodon, Maiasaura, Oviraptor, Psittacosaurus, Spinosaurus, Triceratops, Troodon, Tyrannosaurus rex,* and *Velociraptor* all existed during this period. At the end of the Cretaceous period came a great mass extinction that wiped out the dinosaurs, along with many other groups of animals.

TERTIARY PERIOD

Date: 65 million to 1.8 million years ago
Mammals were extremely diversified at this time, and modern-day creatures such as horses, dogs, cats, bears, and whales developed.

QUATERNARY PERIOD

Date: 1.8 million years ago to today
Temperatures continued to drop during this period. Several periods of glacial development led to what is known as the Ice Age. Prehistoric creatures such as glyptodonts, mammoths, mastodons, *Megatherium,* and saber-toothed cats roamed Earth. A mass extinction of these animals occurred approximately 10,000 years ago. The first human beings evolved during the Quaternary period.

Index

Agnostus, 13
Ampyx, 12
antennae, 4, 10, 21
arthropods, 8–9, *8,* 14, 20, *27*

cephalon, 9, 12, 13, 14, 20, 22, 23, 26

eggs, 20
enrollment, 22, *22*
exoskeleton, *8,* 9, 14–15, 21, 22, 22
eyes, 5, 10, *10,* 13, 15, 18, 21, 26–27

food, 4, 17–18, *19*
fossils, 9, *11,* 16, *16,* 22, 24–26, *25, 27*

legs, 4, 10, 17, *17*
length, 12
lobes, 7, 9

molting, 14–15, 21
mouth, 18

name, 7

paleontologists, 16, 18, 20, 21, 24–26
pygidium, 9, 12, 13, 21, 22, 23

shapes, 13
spines, 12, *12,* 13, *17,* 21, 23

thorax, 9–10, 20
trilobites, *4, 5, 6, 7, 10, 11, 12, 13, 16, 17, 18, 22, 25, 27*

Yoho National Park, *25*

About the Author

Susan H. Gray has bachelor's and master's degrees in zoology and has taught college-level courses in biology. She first fell in love with fossil hunting while studying paleontology in college. In her 25 years as an author, she has written many articles for scientists and researchers, and many science books for children. Susan enjoys gardening, traveling, and playing the piano. She and her husband, Michael, live in Cabot, Arkansas.